Playful
LEARNING
LAB

— FOR —

Kids

Playful
LEARNING LAB
FOR
Kids

**Whole-Body Sensory Adventures to
Enhance Focus, Engagement, and Curiosity**

Claire Heffron
and Lauren Drobnjak

of The Inspired Treehouse

QUARRY

Brimming with creative inspiration, how-to projects, and useful information to enrich your everyday life, Quarto Knows is a favorite destination for those pursing their interests and passions. Visit our site and dig deeper with our books into your area of interest: Quarto Creates, Quarto Cooks, Quarto Homes, Quarto Lives, Quarto Drives, Quarto Explores, Quarto Gifts, or Quarto Kids.

First Published in 2019 by Quarry Books, an imprint of The Quarto Group,
100 Cummings Center, Suite 265-D, Beverly, MA 01915, USA.
T (978) 282-9590 F (978) 283-2742 QuartoKnows.com

Quarry Books titles are also available at discount for retail, wholesale, promotional, and bulk purchase. For details, contact the Special Sales Manager by email at specialsales@quarto.com or by mail at The Quarto Group, Attn: Special Sales Manager, 401 Second Avenue North, Suite 310, Minneapolis, MN 55401, USA.

10 9 8 7 6 5 4 3 2 1

ISBN: 978-1-63159-556-1

Digital edition published in 2019
eISBN: 978-1-63159-557-8

Library of Congress Cataloging-in-Publication Data available

Design: Samantha J. Bednarek
Photography: Lauren McNulty

Printed in China

This book it dedicated to the kids of The Treehouse and their families.
We are grateful for their love and support as we teach kids the power of play.

Contents

Introduction

AS SCHOOL-BASED THERAPISTS, we can count on hearing questions like these almost every single day...

How can we get kids to focus, pay attention, and engage in the classroom?

Why can't kids these days just listen and sit still?

But if there's one thing we've come to understand, it's that learning actually has very little to do with sitting still and a lot more to do with sensory experiences.

Today's kids are getting less stimulation of their vestibular and proprioceptive systems—the sensory systems related to movement—than ever before. Higher academic expectations, testing, and assessments often mean more time sitting at desks, not to mention the trend toward more sedentary play activities, such as video games, computers, and tablets.

The vestibular system, responsible for balance and awareness of the body's position in space, is stimulated when we swing, ride a bike, or turn upside down. The proprioceptive system, on the other hand, is stimulated by movement against resistance or through impact to the joints and muscles. When we jump, stomp, push, or pull, we stimulate our proprioceptive system. When kids get sufficient input to these "movement senses" through active play, they demonstrate better coordination, stronger spatial and body awareness, increased attention, and improved self-regulation.

When we consider the increase in kids who can't attend, can't stop fidgeting, and aren't equipped with basic developmental skills needed for independence, it's clear that all of this time spent sitting still really adds up.

Kids were meant to move. It's that simple.

What does movement have to do with learning? Everything.

When kids' vestibular and proprioceptive systems are stimulated during movement-based learning activities, they demonstrate more attentive and focused behavior. With hands-on learning opportunities, kids are more engaged and demonstrate better understanding and retention of the concepts we're teaching.

The bottom line is: Pencils and worksheets just don't cut it anymore. We can do better. We have to do better if we want all kids—regardless of their learning style or learning challenges—to succeed in school.

Does it require a little more effort to create lessons and activities that engage all of the senses, especially the vestibular and proprioceptive systems? Definitely. But if you're reading this book, you're up for the challenge. Take learning to the next level by:

→ **Supporting teachers who want to create a culture of whole-body, active learning in their classrooms**

→ **Encouraging therapists who know the benefits of movement and sensory play to bring these concepts into classrooms**

→ **Inspiring parents who want to create enriching play and learning experiences for their kids.**

What are you waiting for? Let's get moving and learning!

SENSORY ADVENTURES *for Reading, Literacy, and Language*

KIDS WILL SHAKE THEIR HANDS,
strengthen their core, and move to the rhythm of
words as they explore reading, literacy, and language
through playful activities.

Vocabulary-Building SENSORY SPOTS

→ Kids will love the feel of these tactile sensory spots! This activity is a great way to encourage descriptive vocabulary while promoting body awareness.

MATERIALS

→ 13 pieces of cardboard cut into 12" (30 cm) circles
→ A variety of tactile materials (e.g. shiny craft paper, smooth rocks, foam, bubble wrap, rope, feathers, pompoms, flat-sided marbles, textured fabrics, etc.)
→ Hot glue gun
→ Clock hands from a craft store
→ Brad fastener
→ 2 small metal washers
→ Images of handprints and footprints
→ Non-skid shelf liner

PREPARE FOR YOUR ADVENTURE

Assemble your sensory spots:

1. Cover 12 of the cardboard circles using the tactile materials listed. Use one material to cover two circles **(fig. a)**.

For fabric, paper, bubble wrap, etc., trace a 12" (30 cm) circle onto a material, cut out the circle, and hot glue it to the cardboard. For smooth rocks, feathers, etc., use one hot glue to cover the entire circle in the tactile material.

2. Cut a square of non-skid shelf liner and hot glue it to the bottom of each circle.

Assemble the spinner:

3. Take a sample of each material and hot glue it around the edge of the extra 12" (30 cm) cardboard circle **(fig. b)**.

4. Make a hole through the center of the cardboard circle. Place the clock hand and metal washer onto the brad fastener and push the fastener through the hole. Open the fastener onto the back of the spinner to secure it in place.

5. Glue a handprint or footprint in each quadrant of the spinner.

Fig. a: Cover cardboard circles with tactile materials.

Fig. b: Create a tactile spinner and take turns spinning.

Fig. c: Place the designated body part on the sensory spot.

Fig. d: Describe how the spot feels.

BEGIN YOUR ADVENTURE

6. Ask the kids to take off their shoes and socks to maximize the tactile input.

7. Each kid takes a turn spinning and placing his designated body part on the sensory spot that matches the texture the arrow points to **(fig. c)**.

8. Ask each kid to describe how the sensory spot feels **(fig. d)**.

Maximize the Sensory Experience

→ Talk with the kids about which textures were their favorites. Which textures were harder for them to tolerate on their skin?

→ Use this game to explore spatial concepts and body awareness (e.g. left, right, body parts, top, bottom, under, over, etc.).

OTHER ADVENTURES WITH
Your Sensory Spots

→ Place the spots far apart and have the kids take giant steps to get to each one.

→ Place the spots in a circle, turn on some music, and play a game of musical chairs, using your spots as seats for each kid.

→ Play Duck, Duck, Goose using the spots as designated seats for each kid in the circle.

Sticky WORD TRAP

→ Reinforcing literacy concepts becomes a whole-body experience in this fun, hands-on lab. Kids will also get the added benefit of building hand strength as they fill up their Sticky Word Traps.

MATERIALS
→ Small pieces of paper
→ Pens and pencils
→ Hula hoops
→ Packing tape

PREPARE FOR YOUR ADVENTURE

1. Decide how many sticky word traps to make, based on the literacy concept you would like to address (e.g. long and short vowels, letter sounds, blends, etc.).

2. Make your sticky word traps by stretching pieces of packing tape across the hula hoops, sticky side out **(fig. a)**. The traps will resemble spider webs when you're finished. Label each sticky word trap based on your chosen literacy concept.

3. Write target words on the small pieces of paper **(fig. b)**.

BEGIN YOUR ADVENTURE

For this activity, we'll use the example of long and short vowel sounds as our literacy concept.

4. Have kids select a piece of paper, read the word, and verbally identify whether it has a long or short vowel sound **(fig. c)**.

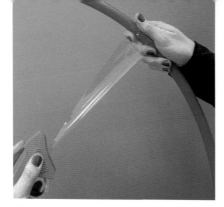

Fig. a: Stretch pieces of packing tape across hula hoops.

Fig. b: Write words on cards or pieces of paper.

Fig. c: Have kids read the words on the cards.

Fig. d: Have them crumple the paper and stick it to the trap.

5. Show them how to crumple the papers in their hands and stick them to the word trap with the corresponding label **(fig. d)**.

Something to Think About

→ This activity appeals to the tactile system and boosts language and literacy skills, but it's also an awesome hand strengthener! Crumpling paper is a great way to build the small muscles of the hands that kids rely on for grasping pencils, cutting with scissors, and tying their shoes.

Maximize the Sensory Experience

→ Place hula hoops at different heights to provide vestibular input through bending and reaching.

→ Incorporate other movements by instructing kids to hop, skip, jump, or gallop to the word traps.

→ Make this into an obstacle course for kids to navigate before sticking their word to the correct word trap.

OTHER ADVENTURES WITH
Your Word Traps

→ Use this activity to address other learning concepts (e.g. animal habitats, letter/sound blends, beginning or ending letter sounds, etc.).

→ Use actual objects, like small toys, figurines, or manipulatives, to sort into the different webs instead of paper.

Spelling Grid JUMPING

→ A simple grid drawn on pavement becomes the backdrop for this awesome, whole-body spelling activity that can be used with kids of all ages and ability levels.

MATERIALS

→ 2 colors of sidewalk chalk
→ Words to spell
   (e.g. kids' names, a spelling list)

PREPARE FOR YOUR ADVENTURE

1. Draw a grid on the concrete with 30 squares (6 rows of 5 squares) with one color of chalk **(fig. a)**.

2. Using the other chalk color, fill each square of the grid with a different letter of the alphabet. Repeat vowels as necessary to fill in the grid.

BEGIN YOUR ADVENTURE

3. Have kids take turns spelling out words. Tell the first kid which word to spell **(fig. b)**.

4. Have him jump to the first letter, and then to each consecutive letter to spell the word **(fig. c)**.

Fig. a: Draw a grid on the concrete and put a letter in each square.

Fig. b: Provide each kid with a word.

Fig. c: Have the kids jump to each letter on the grid to spell the word.

5. When he is done spelling, have him jump out of the grid to wait for his next word.

Maximize the Sensory Experience

→ Explore proprioception by having kids jump higher, lower, harder, and softer.

→ Increase the vestibular input by having kids move in a specific direction (e.g. sideways, back and forth, etc.).

→ Provide a challenge to the auditory system by giving kids a letter sound to jump to.

OTHER ADVENTURES WITH
the Spelling Grid

→ For younger kids who are just learning to recognize the letters in their names, write the letters of their names in the grid with each letter right next to each other.

→ Practice other gross motor skills for moving through the grid (e.g. hop, wheelbarrow walk, crawl, etc.)

LAB 4

Secret Code MOVEMENT

→ Create a secret code with movement! Kids will love spelling out words in a whole new way with this fun lab.

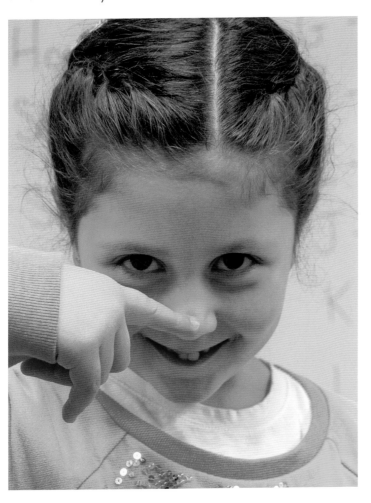

MATERIALS
→ Large marker board/chalkboard
→ Markers/chalk
→ Pen
→ Index cards
→ Paper
→ Pencils

PREPARE FOR YOUR ADVENTURE

1. Work as a team to create a secret movement code by assigning a different movement for each letter of the alphabet.

2. Write the movements on the chalkboard or marker board under each corresponding letter. Examples of movements to use in your code:
- jump
- hop on one foot
- jumping jack
- spin
- clap
- stomp foot
- touch toes
- stand on toes
- march in place
- run in place
- drum on desk
- tap knees
- tap stomach

3. Write several sight words on index card.

Fig. a: Have kids pick a word card.

Fig. b: Use the secret code to perform a movement for each letter of the word.

BEGIN YOUR ADVENTURE

4. Give a sight word card to each kid **(fig. a)**.

5. Have one kid stand in front of the rest of the group and use the secret code to act out his word by performing a different movement for each letter **(fig. b)**.

6. Have the rest of the kids write down each letter on their papers as they decipher them using the code written on the board **(fig. c)**.

7. See who can guess what the word is before the kid is finished acting out the movements.

Fig. c: By watching the movements, other kids decipher and write down each letter.

Maximize the Sensory Experience

→ Have kids act out the movements for a word and challenge the rest of the group to figure out what the word is without writing it down as they go.

→ Reverse the game and have kids spell out a sight word, having the rest of the group act out the corresponding movements.

OTHER ADVENTURES WITH Your Secret Code

→ For younger kids, have them practice using the secret code to spell their names.

→ Work on other concepts with your code. For example, to target the concept of opposites, show kids a word and have them act out the movements to spell the word that is the opposite of the presented word.

Core Strength RHYMING

→ Strong core muscles form the foundation for nearly everything kids need to do throughout the day, from playing on the playground to sitting still in their seats in the classroom. This lab targets those core muscles while reinforcing rhyming skills.

MATERIALS

→ Large exercise ball that is big enough for kids to lie on
→ Pictures of objects (e.g. animals, household objects, etc.)

PREPARE FOR YOUR ADVENTURE

1. Place the ball in an open space that is near one wall.

2. Tape the pictures of the objects to the wall in front of the ball.

3. Have the kid lie with his back on the ball (**fig. a**).

4. Hold the kid's feet or assign a partner to each kid for this job.

BEGIN YOUR ADVENTURE

5. Explain that you will be asking the child to lie down on his back on top of the ball and listen for a word to be called out.

6. Once he hears the word, he has to sit up and point to the picture that corresponds to the word that

Fig. a: Instruct the child to lie down on his back on top of the ball.

Fig. b: When he hears a word, he will sit up and point to an object that rhymes with the word.

rhymes with the word that you called out **(fig. b)**. For example, you say bat and he sits up and points to the picture of a cat.

7. After pointing to the correct word, he lies back down over the ball and waits for the next word.

Maximize the Sensory Experience

→ Use a textured ball to add to the tactile experience of this activity.

→ Enhance the core strengthening, vestibular, and visual motor benefits by having the kid bounce on the ball as he searches for the picture that corresponds to the word.

OTHER ADVENTURES WITH
Your Core Strength Rhyming Lab

→ Instead of pictures, use words on the wall.

→ Complete the activity the same way, but have the kid lie on his belly for different vestibular input and to strengthen the back extensors.

SYLLABLE *Secret* Handshake

→ In this creative lab, kids work with a partner to clap out their own special handshake. In the process, they will gain a better understanding of how many syllables are in different words.

MATERIALS

→ **Word lists containing words with different numbers of syllables**
→ **Pencils**

PREPARE FOR YOUR ADVENTURE

1. Assign a partner to each kid.

2. Have kids experiment with creating different ways of clapping and touching their hands together **(fig. a)**. Demonstrate and give examples such as:

- High five with both hands, fingers pointing up

- One partner puts both hands facing up in front of them and the other partner claps both hands down on top

- Bump both fists together on the knuckles

- Both partners make fists and one partner's fists come down on top of the other's

Fig. a: Practice different ways of clapping and touching hands together.

Fig. b: Clap out the syllables of the words using different movements.

Fig. c: Write numbers to show how many syllables are in each word.

BEGIN YOUR ADVENTURE

3. Provide a word list to each set of partners.

4. Have each set of partners decide how they will clap out the syllables of the words as a team. They can use one style of clapping or combine different styles to make their own secret handshake **(fig. b)**.

5. Have the kids work through the word lists, clapping out the syllables of the words with their partners and writing the number of syllables next to each word **(fig. c)**.

Maximize the Sensory Experience

→ Have kids add other body parts into their handshakes (e.g. stomping feet, bumping elbows, slapping hands on knees, etc.).

→ Have other kids listen to each set of secret handshakes, count the syllables, and come up with another word with the same number of syllables.

OTHER ADVENTURES WITH Secret Handshakes

→ Use this same movement activity to introduce other concepts. For example, give kids a number and ask them to practice counting with one-to-one correspondence by counting each clap up to the designated number.

→ Use this activity to reinforce spelling by having kids clap out each letter of the word as they say the letters aloud.

SENSORY BIN Letter Tracing

→ Forget pencils and paper. Letter tracing comes to life in this lab as kids practice in a tray of colorful sand.

MATERIALS

→ Shallow tray or box
→ Sensory bin filler (salt, sand, dry rice, etc.)
→ Paper
→ Pencil with eraser, marker with cap, or cotton swab
→ Cards with letters printed on them

PREPARE FOR YOUR ADVENTURE

1. Place the paper on the bottom of the tray or box.

2. Pour the sensory bin filler into the tray or box to cover the paper.

BEGIN YOUR ADVENTURE

3. Display one of the letter cards near the sensory bin (**fig. a**).

4. Tell kids to make the letter by tracing their fingers, the eraser end of a pencil, a cotton swab, or a capped marker through the sensory bin filler, displaying the paper underneath (**figs. b and c**).

Fig. a: Display a letter card near the sensory bin.

Fig. b: Use a finger to the trace the letter in the sand.

Fig. c: Try using other tools to trace letters.

Fig. d: When finished, erase the letter and choose a new letter card.

5. Have kids use their hands to erase each letter when they are finished by spreading the sensory bin filler evenly across the tray **(fig. d)**.

6. Repeat with the next letter.

Maximize the Sensory Experience

→ Enhance the tactile experience by trying this activity using textured craft paper at the bottom of the sensory bin.

→ Try increasing the visual contrast by choosing a sensory bin filler and craft paper with highly contrasting colors (e.g. dry black beans as a filler and white or yellow paper at the bottom of the bin).

OTHER ADVENTURES WITH
Letter Tracing

→ Say different words aloud and have kids trace the beginning letter sound or ending letter sound in the sensory bin.

→ Use the sensory bin to practice tracing numbers. Have kids count a quantity of manipulatives or objects, and then trace the corresponding number in the sensory bin.

Letter Formation VISUAL TARGET

→ Using tangible targets as starting and ending points is a novel way to work on early writing skills and can support visual attention and visual motor skills.

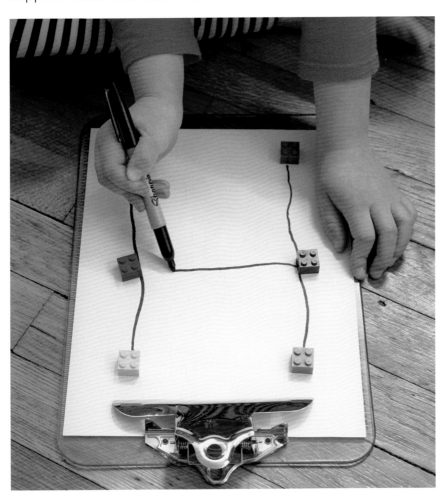

MATERIALS

→ Small stickers, objects, or manipulatives (e.g. buttons, flat-sided marbles, wood or foam shapes, etc.)
→ Dry erase board or clipboard with paper
→ Dry erase markers or markers/crayons

PREPARE FOR YOUR ADVENTURE

1. Place the dry erase board on a flat surface.

2. Place two or more stickers or small objects on the dry erase board.

3. Have kids practice making lines to connect the visual targets on the dry erase board.

BEGIN YOUR ADVENTURE

4. Tell kids which letter they are going to write.

Fig. a: Collect manipulatives to use as targets.

Fig. b: Place manipulatives on paper or dry erase board.

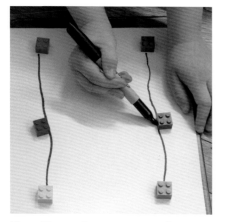

Fig. c: Use marker or crayon to draw lines connecting the manipulatives.

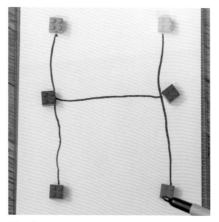

Fig. d: Form letters by connecting the manipulatives.

5. Place the objects on the dry erase board or paper, positioning them so kids can connect the dots to form a letter **(figs. a and b)**.

6. Have kids draw the letter by beginning at one of the visual targets and drawing lines to the rest of the targets until they have formed the letter correctly **(figs. c and d)**.

7. Repeat with the next letter.

Maximize the Sensory Experience

→ Use a vertical magnetic surface with magnets as the visual targets.

→ Call out the color of the target where kids should start or stop (e.g. draw a line from the red sticker to the blue sticker).

→ Create an outline of the letter around the visual targets to provide an enhanced visual cue.

OTHER ADVENTURES WITH
Letter Tracing

→ Use the visual targets to create other shapes and lines on the dry erase board.

→ Use the targets as a multi-step activity by directing kids to draw lines from one target to another in a certain sequence (e.g. draw a line from the blue target to the green target and then to the yellow target).

HIDDEN *Letters*

→ This hands-on lab is a simple way to engage the tactile system and an interesting way to work on letter identification and letter sounds.

MATERIALS
→ Play dough
→ Small letter manipulatives (e.g. beads or magnets)

PREPARE FOR YOUR ADVENTURE

1. Pass out play dough and a handful of letter manipulatives to each kid **(figs. a and b)**.

2. Have kids push letter manipulatives into the play dough to hide them **(fig. c)**.

BEGIN YOUR ADVENTURE

3. Tell kids to squeeze and squish their play dough with their hands to pull out the letters one at a time **(fig. d)**.

Fig. a: Gather play dough and letter manipulatives.

Fig. b: Provide play dough and letters to each child.

Fig. c: Have kids push letter manipulatives into their play dough to hide them.

Fig. d: Kids should pull the letters out of the dough, identifying each one.

4. As they pull out each letter, ask them to identify the letter and say its sound.

Maximize the Sensory Experience

→ Use letter magnets and have kids stand to place them on a vertical magnetic surface as they find each one.

→ Use the same or similar colored letter manipulatives and play dough to increase the visual challenge.

OTHER ADVENTURES WITH
Hidden Letter Lab

→ Give the kids word cards to try to find and match letters.

→ Have kids find the letters of their names and put them in the correct sequence.

→ If you are playing with a group of kids, make it a game and see who can find a specific letter first.

Core Strengthening ALPHABET

→ Working and playing in an all-fours position can be a great way to build core muscle strength. As kids slide their hands across the floor in this lab, they'll boost their core strength while practicing letter formation.

MATERIALS
→ 1 washcloth per kid
→ Smooth floor surface

PREPARE FOR YOUR ADVENTURE

1. Position kids on all fours and put a washcloth under their dominant hand **(fig. a)**.

2. Have kids practice sliding their washcloth across the floor while staying on all fours (e.g. away from their bodies, toward their bodies, in small circles, side to side, etc.).

BEGIN YOUR ADVENTURE

3. Have kids stay in the all-fours position and slide their washcloth to form the letters of the alphabet one at a time on the floor in front of them **(fig. b)**.

4. To maximize the core-strengthening benefits, encourage kids to keep the rest of their body still as they move their hands to form the letters.

Fig. a: In an all-fours position on the floor, place one hand on a washcloth.

Fig. b: Form letters by sliding the washcloth across the floor.

Fig. c: Form letters closer to the body to make the activity easier.

Fig. d: Slide the washcloth out away from the body for more of a challenge.

Maximize the Sensory Experience

→ Have kids try tracing the letters on the floor at different distances from their bodies (closer to the body to make it easier, further from the body for more of a challenge, **(figs. c and d)**.

→ Stick small pieces of tape or stickers on the floor as visual starting and stopping points for the letters.

OTHER ADVENTURES WITH
Core Strengthening Alphabet

→ Have kids make shapes by sliding both hands on the floor.

→ Have kids try to reach visual sight word targets with their washcloths (e.g. stickers or pieces of tape on the floor with sight words written on them), reading the words as they touch them.

Something to Think About
→ Core strength is essential for the progression of nearly all other developmental skills. It's difficult for kids to balance, perform coordinated movements on both sides of the body, sit up straight in a chair, hold a pencil, control scissors, or jump if they don't have strong core muscles.

Why Free Play Matters

STUDIES SAY THAT FREE PLAY may correlate with better executive functioning in kids and that unstructured play is essential for physical, social, and emotional well-being. Studies have also found that people who recall having plenty of free time during childhood enjoy high levels of social success as adults.

There is a time and place for structured, planned learning activities, as well as scheduled, adult-led sports and extracurricular activities. It's also important to allow plenty of time for child-directed activities. Encouraging free play in kids can:

→ Help keep them more engaged in activities they find meaningful for longer periods of time.

→ Help them develop a more spontaneous, dynamic, and functional repertoire of movements and sensory responses that correlate better with real-world experiences than structured, planned exercises or activities.

→ Help them learn ways to tolerate and cope with the unplanned, unexpected sensory, motor, behavioral, social, and cognitive challenges that arise in everyday life.

→ Help adults build an even deeper connection and rapport with students at school and kids at home as they honor and respect the kids' choices, preferences, and interests.

How to increase opportunities for free play

→ Make sure kids have access to the settings, spaces, basic tools, and—above all—time to engage in self-directed play.

→ Trust the idea that simple, self-driven play activities are exactly what help kids develop the motor, sensory, cognitive, and social skills they need most.

→ Give control over to the kids and acknowledge what they're truly capable of. Sit back, be quiet, and watch what happens.

→ Promote more creative play by mixing and matching different toys that the kids don't typically play with at the same time.

→ Try using toys in unusual settings (e.g. take art supplies on your nature walk, build with blocks in the sandbox, etc.).

UNIT

2

EXPLORING MATH
Through the Senses

MATH IS MORE THAN NUMBERS!
Kids will love exploring mathematical concepts
by physically creating angles with their bodies,
jumping like frogs to explore measurement and
bending and stretching to count coins.

Weighted Box CHALLENGE

→ Using colorful, eye-catching materials, kids will put their hands and minds to work to examine the concept of weight in this lab.

MATERIALS

→ 5 similar-sized empty cardboard boxes, appropriate for kids to handle
→ Fillers to add weight to boxes (beanbags, feathers, sand, toys, crayons, beads, rocks, silverware, jingle bells, etc.)
→ Packing tape
→ Bathroom scale
→ Pencil
→ Paper

PREPARE FOR YOUR ADVENTURE

1. Fill each box with a different amount or type of filler. You'll want a range of boxes with different weights.

2. Secure the boxes tightly with tape.

Fig. a: Lift and feel the boxes to put them in order by weight.

Fig. b: Weigh the boxes.

Maximize the Sensory Experience

→ Have kids shake each box and try to guess what's inside.

→ Add even more proprioceptive input and engage core muscles by having a kid lift a box over his head, pass a box around his body, or hold the box out to his right or left.

BEGIN YOUR ADVENTURE

3. Mix the boxes up and spread them out on the floor.

4. Have kids work together to lift and feel the boxes, and then put them in order from lightest to heaviest (**fig. a**).

5. Once the boxes are lined up in order, have kids weigh each one (**fig. b**) and record the weight on a piece of paper, taping it to the outside of each box (**fig. c**).

6. Have kids check to see whether their initial hypothesis was correct. Were the boxes actually in order from lightest to heaviest? If not, have them rearrange based on their findings from the scale.

Fig. c: Record the weight of each box.

OTHER ADVENTURES WITH Weighted Boxes

→ Make a weighted box relay. Have kids stand in line and pass a box over their heads, between their legs, or side to side until all of the boxes have been stacked at the back of the line.

TOUCH and FEEL

→ Using the sense of touch is a great way to examine the features of shapes. Are they curved or pointed? How many sides do they have?

MATERIALS

→ Small items of different shapes (e.g. coin, balloon, crayon, small ball, small book, etc.)
→ Pictures of each item

PREPARE FOR YOUR ADVENTURE

1. Cut a hole in the top of the shoebox so that a kid's hand can fit through and feel what is inside.

2. Place a picture of each item next to the box (**fig. a**).

BEGIN YOUR ADVENTURE

3. Have kids reach into the box and feel around for an object (**fig. b**). No peeking!

4. Have them name and describe each object as they feel it. What shape is it? Is it curved or does it have corners? How many corners or sides does it have?

5. Before pulling the item from the box, have kids look at all of the pictures and see if they can guess which object they are feeling (**fig. c**).

6. Have them pull the object out and see if their guess was correct (**fig. d**).

Fig. a: Place a picture of each item next to the box.

Fig. b: Reach into box and feel for an object.

Fig. c: Have kids point to the picture of the object they think they feel.

Fig. d: Pull the object out of the box to see if they're right.

→ Use different descriptors for each object (e.g. soft, hard, round, square, rough, smooth, etc.)

→ Change up the range of difference between the objects (making the objects very similar or different can make this activity easier or more difficult).

OTHER ADVENTURES WITH
Your Touch and Feel Box

→ Use the Touch and Feel Box for 3D shape identification (e.g. cylinder, sphere, cube, rectangular prism, etc.). Have kids feel an object of each shape in the box, name the shape, and describe its attributes.

Something to Think About
→ This activity involves stereognosis, which is the body's ability to perceive and recognize what an object is without receiving information from the visual or auditory system to help in the identification. It is the tactile system hard at work providing information about texture, size, spatial properties, weight, and temperature.

Body ANGLES

→ Using whole-body movements to explore math helps kids understand and retain concepts. In this lab, kids will get creative to figure out how to form different angles with their bodies.

MATERIALS
→ Marker
→ Index cards
→ An empty container

PREPARE FOR YOUR ADVENTURE

1. Draw obtuse, right, straight, and acute angles on index cards.

2. Discuss the properties of each angle. Right angles are 90 degrees, acute angles are less than 90 degrees, obtuse angles are more than 90 degrees, and straight angles are 180 degrees.

3. Explain to kids that they are going to try to make these angles in various ways with their own bodies. The angle they make will be determined by the card they pull out of the container.

BEGIN YOUR ADVENTURE

4. Choose a piece of paper from the container (**fig. a**).

5. Name and describe the angle.

6. Have kids move their bodies into positions that mimic the angle they chose (**figs. b, c, and d**). Ask them to hold their angles for a count of 5.

Fig. a: Have kids choose a card with an angle printed on it.

Fig. b: Replicate the angle using a part of the body.

Fig. c: Or use the whole body to create the angle.

Fig. d: Try to recreate the angle as closely as possible using the body.

Maximize the Sensory Experience

→ Have one kid pull an angle from the container, and then describe to other kids how to make the angle with their bodies. Can they follow the directions? Do they know which type of angle they made?

→ Increase the vestibular input by having kids try a series of angles (e.g. move from an acute angle/down dog position to a straight angle/standing up tall to a right angle/long sit with arms overhead).

OTHER ADVENTURES WITH
Body Angles

→ Have a kid make an angle with his body and have others guess what type of angle it is.

→ Have kids mimic angles in their environment with their bodies by standing next to them (e.g. stand next to a desk and make a 90-degree angle by bending over at the waist).

Whole Body TIME

→ Telling time is tons of fun as kids become the clock in this creative lab. A couple of simple props is all you need.

MATERIALS
→ **Pool noodle, cut in half**
→ **Poster board**
→ **Marker**

PREPARE FOR YOUR ADVENTURE

1. Cut a pool noodle in half to make two pieces that will serve as the hands of the clock. You can use any similar objects for this activity (two wooden spoons, two dowels rods, etc.)

2. Have the kid practice pointing to the numbers on the clock around her body. 12 o'clock is at her head, 6 o'clock is at her feet.

3. Explain to the kid that she is going to be using the pool noodles to make the hands of the clock as you call out a time.

Fig. a: Call out a time for the kids to replicate.

Fig. b: Have kids replicate the time using the pool noodles.

➜ Use weighted objects, like small medicine balls or cans of soup, to increase the proprioceptive input and strengthening benefits.

➜ Use empty water bottles filled with rice or beans to increase the auditory feedback when completing this activity.

BEGIN YOUR ADVENTURE

4. Call out a time for the kid to replicate using the pool noodle clock hands **(fig. a)**.

5. Have the kid stand facing the poster board with the clock numbers.

6. Have him replicate the time he heard using the pool noodles **(fig. b)**. For instance, if the time on the card reads 3:20, the pool noodle in his left hand will point in the direction of the 3 on a clock face, while the pool noodle in his right hand would point to the 4 to indicate 20 past the hour.

OTHER ADVENTURES WITH
Whole Body Time Lab

➜ Have kids incorporate time sequences into this activity at intervals that you determine. For example, call out the time of 3:00. The kid starts her body at 3:00 and moves in intervals of 20 minutes (3:20, 3:40, 4:00, etc.).

➜ For kids who are just starting to learn the concept of telling time, use only one pool noodle to practice the hour hand or the minute hand by itself.

Something to Think About
➜ This activity involves bilateral coordination and midline crossing, which are important developmental skills that translate into classroom tasks like reading, writing, and using scissors.

Calming Sensory Strategies for Learning

IF YOU STEP BACK AND THINK about school from a kid's perspective, it's easy to see why so many of them have difficulty managing the stress of a school day.

With each new school year, kids face new academic demands and expectations, along with a whole new schedule, which may include different bedtimes, wake-up times, pick-up and drop-off times, and even mealtimes.

Going to school also means adjusting to complex social nuances and managing all different kinds of relationships. Put this all together with some of the most intense sensory input possible—noise in the cafeteria, 25 kids moving around the classroom, school bells, morning announcements—and it's no wonder that kids can feel overwhelmed at school.

The good news is that there are many calming strategies that can be beneficial to support learning and self-regulation in the classroom, during homework time, and beyond. Try offering:

1. A quiet space and a way for the child to signal when she needs a break

2. Calming tactile input, including deep pressure and tactile bins

3. Calming oral sensory input, including chewing gum, chewy snacks, or sucking against resistance

4. Calming auditory input, including white noise or quiet music

5. Calming proprioceptive input, including play activities that require pushing or pulling against resistance

6. Calming vestibular input, including repetitive, rhythmic movements

UNIT

3

Sensory Science EXPLORATIONS

THESE FUN SENSORY ADVENTURES
are perfect for engaging all of the senses
while targeting topics such as light and shadows,
the body, and earth science.

LAB 20

LIGHT AND SHADOW Exploration

→ In this sensory science lab, kids will learn about light and shadow through play. Turn out the lights to get started!

MATERIALS
→ Light source (e.g. flashlight, table lamp, etc.)
→ Everyday household objects (e.g. spoon, hairbrush, toys, etc.)
→ Light colored sheet (optional)

PREPARE FOR YOUR ADVENTURE

1. Turn off the main overhead lights in the room.

2. Set up your light source so you can cast shadows of your objects onto the wall or sheet.

Gather the materials.

Fig. a: Have the child shine the flashlight on an object near the sheet or wall.

BEGIN YOUR ADVENTURE

3. Have the kid close his or her eyes while you choose an object.

4. Project a shadow of the object onto the wall or sheet **(fig. a)**.

5. Have the kid open his eyes and see if he can guess the object by looking only at the shadow **(fig. b)**. No peeking at the object!

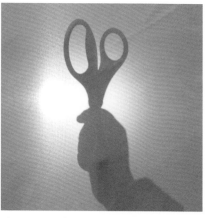
Fig. b: Have friends guess what the object is based on the appearance of the shadow.

Maximize the Sensory Experience

→ Have kids touch each object before you cast the shadow and explain how the object feels. Does the shadow reflect the texture?

→ Explore whole-body movement by casting shadows of kids in different positions (e.g. jumping, reaching overhead, touching toes, holding warrior position, etc.).

OTHER ADVENTURES WITH Shadows

→ Tape a piece of paper to the wall and have the kid try to trace around the shadow using a crayon or marker.

→ See what happens to the shadows as you move the object closer to or further away from the light.

Space ORBIT

→ Bring outer space right into your classroom, therapy room, or living room by teaching kids about orbits in a whole new way.

MATERIALS

→ Sidewalk chalk if playing outside
→ Masking tape if playing indoors

PREPARE FOR YOUR ADVENTURE

1. Talk about the concept of orbits.

2. If playing outside, draw a 2' (0.6 meter) diameter circle on the cement with sidewalk chalk **(fig. a)**.

3. If playing inside, create a 2' (0.6 meter) diameter circle using masking tape.

BEGIN YOUR ADVENTURE

4. Tell kids that the circle represents the sun.

5. Have the kids use their bodies to represent orbits:

- Place hands inside the circle and feet outside the circle **(fig. b)**. Keep hands planted on the floor and walk feet around the perimeter of the circle. Try this facing up (crab walk

Fig. a: Draw a circle on the pavement with chalk.

Fig. b: Keep hands in the circle and move feet around the orbit.

Fig. c: Keep feet in the circle and move hands around the orbit.

position) or facing down (downward-dog position).

- Place feet inside the circle and hands outside the circle **(fig. c)**. Keep feet planted on the floor and walk hands around the perimeter of the circle.

OTHER ADVENTURES WITH
Orbits

→ Write letter sounds, blends, or another category in the middle of the center circle. Write words related to the category around the circle and have kids move their hands or feet to touch each one as they read the words.

→ Write a number in the center of each circle and numbers around the outside of the circle. Have kids walk their hands or feet to two numbers that add up to the center number, saying the math fact aloud (e.g. 10 in the middle of the circle, walk hands to 6 and 4 saying, "6 + 4 = 10").

Maximize the Sensory Experience

→ With your tape or sidewalk chalk, create marks (planets) on the floor or cement around the center circle for kids to use as targets to touch with their hands or feet as they create their orbits.

→ Use different colors to make the marks around the center circle and instruct kids to move their hands or feet to a specific color or sequence of colors.

→ Experiment with creating the orbits at different speeds and with stopping and starting on command.

Earth Science BALLOON

Fig. a: Use a funnel to fill balloons with the different fillers.

Fig. b: Push, squeeze, and squish the items down into the balloon.

→ This lab gives kids the chance to interact with the outdoors in a creative, new way by getting their hands dirty and taking a closer look at nature items.

MATERIALS
→ Peat moss
→ Dirt
→ Pebbles
→ Clay
→ Sand
→ Balloons
→ Funnel

PREPARE FOR YOUR ADVENTURE

1. Set out containers full of each nature item.

2. Provide a balloon to each kid and have kids choose which item they would like to use to fill their balloons.

Fig. c: Squeeze the balloons and guess what's inside.

BEGIN YOUR ADVENTURE

3. Help kids use the funnel to fill their deflated balloons with their chosen nature items **(fig. a)**.

4. Kids will need to squish and squeeze to push the items into the balloons **(fig. b)**.

Maximize the Sensory Experience

Before starting the activity, take kids on a hike so they can gather their own nature items to fill their balloons.

→ Have kids trade balloons and see if they can use their hands to guess which earthy item is inside each one **(fig. c)**.

→ Place the balloons in front of the kids. Call out one of the nature items and challenge kids to find the correct balloon using only their hands.

OTHER ADVENTURES WITH Your Earth Science Balloon

→ Keep your squishy sensory balloons and use them later as fidget tools to keep little hands busy at home or in the classroom.

→ Experiment with filling balloons with other fillers, such as play dough, flour, and marbles.

HANDS-ON Cloud Formation

→ This lab will bring the clouds down to the kids' level, allowing them to explore different cloud formations using their hands.

MATERIALS
→ Hair conditioner
→ Cornstarch
→ Pictures of cloud formations (cirrus, cumulus, stratus, cumulonimbus)

PREPARE FOR YOUR ADVENTURE

1. Pour hair conditioner and cornstarch into a bowl (1 part hair conditioner to 2 parts cornstarch) **(fig. a)**.

2. Have kids mix well with their hands to form dough **(figs. b and c)**.

3. Give a ball of the dough to each kid.

BEGIN YOUR ADVENTURE

4. Provide kids with images of each type of cloud formation.

5. Have kids use their hands to create the different cloud formations using the soft dough **(fig. d)**.

Fig. a: Gather the ingredients and pour them into a bowl.

Fig. b: Mix until a dough starts to form.

Fig. c: Knead with hands until dough comes together.

Fig. d: Use dough to create clouds.

Maximize the Sensory Experience

→ After finishing this lab, save the cloud dough to use in a sensory bin or sensory table.

→ Pair kids with partners. Have one kid create a cloud formation without telling his friend which one he is making. Have the other partner try to guess which formation his partner made.

OTHER ADVENTURES WITH
Your Cloud Dough

→ Have kids use the cloud dough to create different shapes, letters, or numbers.

→ Try making shapes in the cloud dough with cookie cutters.

HOMEMADE *Butter*

→ All you need is some moving and shaking to turn a liquid into a solid (and make a tasty treat) in this simple science lab.

MATERIALS
→ A clean jar with a lid
→ Heavy cream

PREPARE FOR YOUR ADVENTURE

1. Clean out a small jar (e.g. baby food jar, jelly jar, etc.).

2. Pour a small amount of heavy cream into the jar **(fig. a)**. The more you use, the longer the process will take.

3. Secure the lid to the jar **(fig. b)**.

BEGIN YOUR ADVENTURE

4. Talk to kids about where their food comes from and how it's made.

5. Instruct kids that they will be holding on tightly to the jar and shaking it to turn the heavy cream into butter.

6. Have kids shake the jar and observe the contents as the liquid changes **(fig. c)**.

Fig. a: Pour cream into the jar.

Fig. b: Screw the lid tightly onto the jar.

Maximize the Sensory Experience

→ Instruct kids to hold the jar using both hands for added midline crossing and bilateral coordination.

→ Have kids shake the jar in different ways (e.g. fast, slow, high, low, side to side, etc.).

Fig. c: Shake the jar and observe the changes.

Fig. d: Enjoy the butter!

OTHER ADVENTURES WITH
Homemade Butter

→ Have kids spread their butter on a warm piece of toast (**fig. d**) and watch the solid butter change back into a liquid.

→ Try other liquid-to-solid experiments by making gelatin, pudding, or play dough.

Animal SLEEPOVER

→ Some animals have pretty interesting ways of sleeping— standing up, upside down, even side by side. In this lab, kids will explore how animals say goodnight.

MATERIALS
→ Sheets
→ Blankets
→ Pillows
→ Mat, couch, bed, or mattress

PREPARE FOR YOUR ADVENTURE

1. Find a soft, comfortable space to play, such as a bed, mat, couch, or mattress.

2. Gather sheets, blankets, and pillows near the play space.

BEGIN YOUR ADVENTURE

• **Rabbits** sleep in a hole. Have the child crouch or sit on the mat/bed and build a rabbit hole around him, using blankets and pillows until only his face is visible.

• **Mallard ducks** team up, sleeping in rows to protect themselves from predators. Sit side by side on the mat/bed and link arms **(fig. a)**. Pretend to sway and rock in the water with arms linked and eyes closed.

• **Birds** sleep in nests. Build your own nest by winding blankets and sheets into a circular shape with a space in the middle to climb inside.

• **Otters** sleep in the water without floating away by wrapping themselves in kelp and seaweed. Wrap kids' bodies in sheets and blankets, and then pretend to float in the water by rocking from side to side **(fig. b)**.

• **Bats** sleep mostly during the day, hanging from their feet on tree branches or rocks. Have kids try lying on the bed with their heads tipped off the side so they are upside down **(fig. c)**.

• **Flamingoes** can sleep while standing on one leg. Try standing on one foot and closing your eyes **(fig. d)**.

Fig. a: Find a friend and try sleeping like a duck.

Fig. b: Wrap up in a blanket to sleep like an otter.

Maximize the Sensory Experience

→ Change the tactile and proprioceptive experience by using heavy quilts, down comforters, or lightweight sheets.

Fig. c: Try sleeping upside down like a bat.

Fig. d: Stand on one foot to sleep like a flamingo.

OTHER ADVENTURES WITH

Animal Sleepover

→ Ask one kid to mimic one of the sleeping animals above while the others try to guess what animal he might be.

→ Add in some fun animal facts. Where is each animal found on the globe?

Something to Think About

→ This activity is a great way to explore deep pressure and repetitive, rhythmic movement as calming sensory strategies at bedtime or any time of day. Activities like bear hugs, rocking, rolling, and swinging can all provide tactile and vestibular input that calms kids' sensory systems.

How the Environment Shapes the Way Kids Play

PLAY IS THE PRIMARY OCCUPATION of childhood and the single most significant contributor to healthy development skills. From language to motor to cognitive development and everything in between, play is the catalyst for kids to practice every skill they'll need to grow into independent, fully functioning individuals.

Research has shown that kids' environments can help determine how kids play. Some of the most important environmental factors to consider are the following.

The Size of the Play Space

Large, wide-open spaces lead to more physically active play, while small, tight spaces tend to encourage more imaginative, dramatic play.

We can use this knowledge to design learning, play, and therapeutic experiences for kids. We can facilitate the development of gross motor skills by moving play-based treatment sessions to the playground or gym. We can encourage social skills and imaginative play by incorporating opportunities for kids to interact in smaller play spaces such as tents and forts.

The Social Environment

A sense of safety and security is crucial for kids and helps them to feel free to explore and engage with the materials and people in their surroundings.

Having a familiar adult present can boost a child's sense of security; however, studies show that adults in the play space means less physically active play.

The Sensory Features of the Environment

Children have their own unique sensory preferences and needs, which impact every area of development, including play. Sensory features of a space include visual and auditory distractions, tactile items to explore, lighting, smells, and equipment and space for movement play.

Familiarity or Novelty of Space and Materials

Kids are naturally drawn to novelty. Novel toys and play items can add to the complexity of kids' play. Rotating and planning which materials are available can influence how kids interact with the play items. However, kids also need time to become familiar with using toys and play items before they will play in an engaged and developmentally beneficial manner.

Complexity and Variety of Space and Materials

Simple, less-detailed, and more open-ended materials tend to promote more imaginative and dramatic play.

When it comes to gross motor play, a variety of materials appears to be one of the most important factors. Adding moveable, gross-motor manipulatives to open spaces, such as balls, beanbags, streamers, hula hoops, and stepping stones, creates more flexible and variable movement-based play and promotes more physical activity overall than static play equipment.

A larger variety of play behaviors can be seen in kids when the play environment has diverse and interesting physical features. Outdoor play is perfect for this.

Whether kids are engaged in independent, free play or more structured activities, the environment can truly shape the way kids play and interact.

UNIT

4

Sensory Social Studies ADVENTURES

BREATHE NEW LIFE
into common social studies topics such as teamwork,
social skills, emotions, and transportation with these
movement-infused sensory adventures.

Rabbit HOLE

→ Imagination is key in this fun group-movement challenge. Kids will have to figure out how to work together to fit everyone into a small space.

MATERIALS
→ Hula hoop
→ Four plastic cups, all the same height

PREPARE FOR YOUR ADVENTURE

1. Find an open space to play.

2. At one end of your play space, balance the hula hoop on top of the overturned cups so that it is elevated off the ground **(fig. a)**.

3. Have kids practice stepping into and out of the raised hula hoop without knocking it off the cups.

BEGIN YOUR ADVENTURE

4. Lay the pretend-play foundation for the game by telling the group of kids they are rabbits, and they have to get into their rabbit hole (the hula hoop) before the fox finds them.

Fig. a: Set the hula hoop on top of the cups.

Fig b: As they play, kids have to step carefully into the hoop.

5. To get into their hole, the rabbits must step carefully over the hula hoop without knocking it off of the cups **(fig. b)**. How many rabbits can fit inside the hole?

OTHER ADVENTURES WITH

Rabbit Hole

→ Make it into a game of tag. Assign one person to be the fox. Begin the game of tag, using the hula hoop as a home base where the rabbits are safe (they can't be tagged). If the hoop gets knocked down, a new person becomes the fox.

→ Promote cooperation and problem-solving skills by having a group of kids hold hands and figure out how to get in and out of the rabbit hole without breaking the chain or knocking down the hoop.

Maximize the Sensory Experience

→ Have kids try to navigate to the rabbit hole with their eyes closed by listening to verbal directions from a friend or adult (e.g. walk forward three steps and step over the hula hoop).

→ Introduce a discussion about body space. How did kids feel when they were crammed inside the hole, very close to others? What does appropriate body space look like during a game vs. in the classroom vs. during social interactions?

→ Raise the hoop a little farther off the ground and have kids enter the hole by crawling under the hoop instead of stepping in.

Who's MISSING?

→ The bigger the group of kids, the greater the challenge will be in this playful, social-studies lab. This is an especially fun game for new groups of kids who are just getting to know each other.

Fig. a: Have kids sit in a group with their eyes closed.

Fig. b: One child is chosen to leave the group.

Maximize the Sensory Experience

→ Add an auditory element. Have kids keep their eyes closed after the child leaves. Have each kid in the group say hello. Can kids guess who is missing based on the voices?

MATERIALS

→ Group of kids

PREPARE FOR YOUR ADVENTURE

Have the whole group of kids sit in a circle. Encourage everyone to take a moment to look at each person in the group.

BEGIN YOUR ADVENTURE

1. Tell the group that on the count of three, everyone will close and/or cover his or her eyes **(fig. a)**, and an adult will tap one child on the shoulder **(fig. b)**.

2. Tell the kids that if they are tapped on the shoulder, they should quickly and quietly stand up and walk to a designated spot in another room.

Fig. c: When the remaining kids open their eyes, can they guess who is missing?

3. Count to three again and have everyone open their eyes. The kids then look around the room and try to guess who is missing **(fig. c)**.

OTHER ADVENTURES WITH Memory

→ Set up a center in the classroom with photos of students as a follow-up to playing the live game.

→ Play using photos of family members or friends. Help your kids get to know people in school with photos of the custodian, secretary, principal, music teacher, etc.

→ Change it up and play What's Missing with household items. Cover the items, secretly remove one, and then see if the kids can guess which is gone.

TRACE ME

→ Whether they're getting to know new friends or surrounded by familiar faces, this lab encourages kids to work together and learn more about each other.

MATERIALS

→ **Chalk, crayons, or markers**
→ **Large roll of paper or a concrete surface**

PREPARE FOR YOUR ADVENTURE

1. Find an open indoor or outdoor space to play.

2. Use chalk if playing outside or large paper with crayons and markers if playing inside.

BEGIN YOUR ADVENTURE

3. Have a kid lie, face up, on the surface (paper or concrete) while another kid traces around the outline of his body **(fig. a)**.

4. Once the kid's entire body is traced, have him stand up **(fig. b)**.

5. Have every kid take a turn being traced.

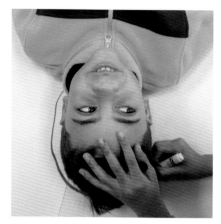

Fig. a: Take turns tracing friends' bodies.

Fig. b: When tracings are complete, stand up.

Fig. c: Fill in the details of friends' facial features.

Fig. d: Add more details like clothes and shoes.

6. Next, have kids draw in the details of their friends, including faces, hair, clothing, facial expressions, jewelry, shoes, etc. **(figs. c and d)**.

Maximize the Sensory Experience

→ Add an auditory element to the game by having kids call out the features to draw on a friend's traced body (e.g. blue shoes, a green shirt, a pink bow in her hair, etc.).

→ Add to the tactile experience by using fabric with different textures, beads, ribbon, and other art supplies to decorate the drawings.

OTHER ADVENTURES WITH
Body Tracing

→ Have kids draw in attributes of community helpers on their friends' traced bodies. Add a badge for a policeman, a fire chief hat, a mail bag, etc.

→ Have kids trace other objects on the paper or concrete. Remove the objects and see if their friends can guess what they've traced.

EMOTION Exploration

→ Identifying and describing emotions (as well as the things that cause kids to feel different emotions) is a great way to support self-regulation. You can help kids develop the skills they need to be good friends and community members.

MATERIALS

→ Cards with images of faces displaying different emotions (happy, sad, afraid, surprised, angry, etc.)

PREPARE FOR YOUR ADVENTURE

1. Make cards with printed or cut-out pictures of faces with different emotions.

2. Find an open space to play.

3. Scatter the cards around the open space with the images face down **(fig. a)**.

BEGIN YOUR ADVENTURE

4. Explain to the kids that they will move around the room as instructed (skip, hop, jump, crawl, walk, etc.). When you say stop, they will find the closest card and pick it up **(fig. b)**.

5. The kids will look at their selected cards and determine what emotion is represented. They will replicate the emotion with their own faces.

6. When asked about the emotions they are displaying, the kids will name the emotion (happy, sad, afraid, surprised, angry, etc.) and describe a

Fig. a: Scatter emotion cards face down on the floor.

Fig. b: Have kids move around the room in different ways to choose a card.

scenario that would make them feel that emotion (e.g. "I get angry when my sister takes my clothes.").

7. The game continues until the kids have explored all of the emotions.

Maximize the Sensory Experience

→ Talk about the sensory systems that might be affected with each emotion. For example, "When you are angry, how do you feel?" They may give answers like hot, shaky, etc.

→ Have kids use their bodies to show each emotion in a different way (e.g. jumping up and down to show excitement, stomping foot to show anger, etc.).

OTHER ADVENTURES WITH
Exploring Emotions

→ Add a literacy component by writing the words that describe each emotion instead of using pictures on the cards.

→ Talk about synonyms and antonyms with emotions. What is a synonym for happy? How about delighted?

TRANSPORTATION Cutting

→ In this hands-on lab, kids use their visual skills to sort through the colorful cards, matching vehicles to the correct paths. Then, they'll get some scissor-skill practice as they move their scissors along the roads.

MATERIALS
→ Cardstock
→ Colored tape
→ Thin permanent marker or pen
→ Scissors
→ Container

PREPARE FOR YOUR ADVENTURE

1. Place lines of tape onto the cards and draw details on the tape to represent the paths that correspond with different vehicles (e.g. clouds for an airplane, tracks for a train, stars for a spaceship, waves for a boat, road lines for a car, etc.) **(fig. a)**.

2. Draw the corresponding vehicles onto several small pieces of tape **(fig. b)**.

3. Shuffle the cards and put them into a container.

Fig. a: Place lines of colored tape onto cards and draw details on the lines of tape.

Fig. b: Draw vehicles on small pieces of tape and place one on each kid's thumb.

Maximize the Sensory Experience

→ Use thicker paper or textured paper for increased proprioceptive feedback.

→ Use tape and paper that have high visual contrast to make the tape lines stand out.

BEGIN YOUR ADVENTURE

4. Place a piece of tape with a vehicle drawn on it around each kid's thumb.

5. Tell each kid to look in the container to find the card with the path that matches the vehicle on his thumb.

6. When he finds the matching card, have him grasp his scissors and cut along the tape line in order to drive his vehicle along the road, track, or other pathway **(fig. c)**.

7. Repeat until the kids have used all of the cards.

Fig. c: Have kids find the card with the path that matches their vehicle and cut down the path.

OTHER ADVENTURES WITH
Transportation Cutting

→ Use the tape to create roads of different shapes on each card in order to give kids practice cutting out triangles, squares, etc.

→ Create roads that have turns and zigzags by placing the tape on the paper at different angles.

ROAD SIGN VISUAL Magnet Maze

→ Stop or go? Fast or slow? Kids will get to practice all of these and more with this hands-on lab that teaches all about road signs.

MATERIALS
→ Paper plate
→ Small magnets
→ Markers
→ Small road sign cutouts (stop signs, do not enter signs, red light, green light, yellow light, intersection sign, yield sign)
→ Small picture of a car
→ Craft stick

PREPARE FOR YOUR ADVENTURE

1. Draw a simple maze on the paper plate, adding details to make it look like roads.

2. Glue road signs along the roads.

3. Glue the car to one magnet and place it on the road.

4. Glue another magnet to a craft stick.

Gather the materials.

Fig. a: Draw roads and use the magnet to move the car around the roads.

BEGIN YOUR ADVENTURE

5. Have a kid hold the craft stick with the magnet on the bottom of the plate, under the car magnet.

6. Have her move the craft stick under the plate in order to move the car along the road **(fig. a)**.

7. When she reaches a road sign or light, have her identify it and make the car obey the road sign.

Maximize the Sensory Experience

→ Call out a road sign for kids to find and have them drive their cars to that specific sign.

→ Call out a series of signs to see if kids can remember the sequence and drive their cars to the signs in the correct order.

OTHER WAYS TO PLAY WITH

the Visual Magnet Maze

→ For younger kids, simply use the road signs as targets and have them drive their cars from sign to sign.

→ Make roads of different shapes on the plate, or create roads in the shapes of different letters so kids can use their magnet cars to trace the letters.

Creating a Sensory-Friendly Learning Environment

PLAY IS ONE OF THE BEST WAYS to ensure that kids get the exposure they need to movement and other sensory experiences. It can be hard to think of ways to build play and sensory input into a traditional classroom setting, but it's so important to engage the entire sensory system to help kids learn and function at their best. There are many creative ways to transform typical activities to make learning accessible to all students.

Some kids need an extra dose of movement for concepts to really sink in. Others respond best when material is introduced through music. Still others need a hands-on approach—they need to manipulate objects, build things, and take things apart. And some kids may need less sensory input to stay focused and attentive.

Here are several common classroom activities and examples of how to give them an extra dose of play.

Journals and Handwriting
→ Allow kids to write in different positions—on the floor, in a beanbag chair, standing with work taped to the wall, or even lying under a table with their work taped to the underside.

→ Listen to a story on headphones and draw a picture.

→ Practice letter formation in a sand or salt tray with colored paper at the bottom. Or, use a wiggle pen.

Flashcards
→ Place flashcards out on the floor and have kids stomp or jump on each one as they give you the answer. Or, put them on a table and have kids slap the answer.

→ Hide cards in a tactile bin. Kids can dig for answers.

Quiet Reading
→ Turn off the lights and give each child a flashlight.

→ Allow kids to chew gum or have a snack while reading.

Lecture Instruction
→ Embed whole-body movements during circle time (e.g. stomp out the days of the week, jump out the months of the year, use different movements to accompany letter sounds, etc.).

→ Present concepts using music, rhymes, and rhythms.

→ Introduce material with video or other multimedia.

→ Introduce manipulatives and/or objects related to the lesson that the kids can pass around.

Worksheets
→ Laminate worksheets and then provide small, laminated cards with answers so kids can use them to fill in the blanks.

→ Let kids work with colored dry erase markers on laminated worksheets.

UNIT

5

ACTIVE SENSORY
Art Activities

ART CAN BE FASCINATING
when it is created in a space outside of a piece
of paper. Kids will use all of their senses to create
beautiful bubble art, mix colors in shaving cream, and
make a unique collage of sticky notes.

Partner PAINTING

→ Kids will make a friend and a masterpiece in this cooperative art lab. This activity is a great way to target visual-motor and fine-motor skills as kids play an artsy game of follow the leader.

MATERIALS

→ Paint, crayons, or markers
→ Drawing paper

PREPARE FOR YOUR ADVENTURE

1. Match each kid with a partner.

2. Provide each kid with paper and drawing/painting utensils.

3. Designate one kid as the leader and one as the follower for each set of partners.

BEGIN YOUR ADVENTURE

4. The leader will draw or paint a picture slowly, one step at a time **(fig. a)**.

5. The follower watches and duplicates each step of the drawing or painting onto his own paper to make an exact replica of the leader's drawing **(fig. b)**.

Fig. a: One kid acts as the leader while the other kid watches.

Fig. b: The follower replicates each detail the leader makes on the paper.

6. Set a timer and when it rings, compare the two drawings **(fig. c)**. Do they look exactly the same?

7. Have the kids switch roles so the leader becomes the follower.

Fig. c: Compare pictures to see if they look exactly alike.

Maximize the Sensory Experience

→ Tape the paper onto a wall or another vertical surface for additional strengthening, sensory, and motor benefits.

→ Take the visual system out of the activity. Have the leader describe what he is drawing without showing it to his partner. Challenge the partner to carry out the instructions, and then compare the two drawings at the end.

OTHER ADVENTURES WITH
Partner Painting

→ Play with a group. Position one kid (the leader) at an easel or marker board at the front of the group. Have him create a drawing or painting as the rest of the kids imitate it on their own small marker boards or pieces of paper.

→ Take the activity outside and try partner drawing using sidewalk chalk.

LAB 34

BUBBLE Painting

→ This lab takes blowing bubbles to a whole new level as kids use their own breath and some soapy suds to create colorful prints on paper.

MATERIALS
- → Watercolor paper
- → Food coloring
- → Dish soap
- → Cup
- → Straws
- → Large container or tray
- → Water

PREPARE FOR YOUR ADVENTURE

1. Squirt some dish soap into the bottom of the cup **(fig. a)**.

2. Fill the cup with about 2 inches (5 cm) of water **(fig. b)**.

3. Put the end of one straw inside the end of another straw to make one long straw.

4. Place the cup on top of a tray or inside a larger container.

BEGIN YOUR ADVENTURE

5. Place one end of the straw into the water in the cup.

6. Have kids blow gently, but constantly, into the water to create bubbles **(fig. c)**.

7. When the bubbles reach the top of the cup, drop a couple of drops of food coloring on top **(fig. d)**.

8. Have kids continue blowing into the straw while you hold the watercolor paper on top of the bubbles **(fig. e)**. The bubbles will stain the paper as they begin to spill over the side of the cup and into the container.

9. Continue to add drops of food coloring as the bubbles continue to spill over the sides of the cup.

10. Scrape away any leftover bubbles from the paper and lay flat to dry **(fig. f)**.

Fig. a: Put soap into the bottom of the cup.

Fig. b: Pour water into the cup.

Fig. c: Blow bubbles using the straw.

Fig. d: Squeeze food coloring onto the bubbles.

Fig. e: Place watercolor paper on top of the bubbles.

Fig. f: Create colorful prints using the bubbles.

Maximize the Sensory Experience

→ Add a drop of essential oil to the mixture to provide a calming or alerting smell.

→ Have kids hum while they blow bubbles into the straw for vibration and auditory input.

OTHER WAYS TO PLAY WITH
Bubble Painting

→ Add drops of two different colors to the same container of bubbles to see what the color combinations look like on the paper.

→ Try this activity as a team. Make one large bowl of bubbles for a group of kids to blow into together, each printing their own piece of watercolor paper as they go.

LAB 35

Tape Collage ART

→ Build interest and engagement by working with tape. This art lab is also great for supporting fine-motor development and hand strength.

MATERIALS

→ Tape (duct tape, washi tape, painter's tape, masking tape, etc.)
→ Construction paper
→ Crayon or marker

PREPARE FOR YOUR ADVENTURE

1. Write each kid's name on construction paper with crayon or marker (**fig. a**).

2. Place small pieces of tape on a table or another surface.

BEGIN YOUR ADVENTURE

3. Have kids peel tape pieces off of the surface (**fig. b**) and place them, one by one, along the lines to spell their names.

4. Have them continue to tear and place the tape until all lines are covered (**fig. c**).

Gather the materials.

Fig. a: Write a kid's name on the paper.

Fig. b: Have kids peel off small pieces of tape.

Fig. c: Place the pieces of tape on the lines of each letter.

Maximize the Sensory Experience

→ Try this activity using different writing fonts (e.g. cursive, block letters, etc.) to make the visual challenge more difficult.

→ Have an adult tear tape pieces and place them all over the table so that the kids have to use their fine-motor strength and grasping skills, as well as their visual-motor skills, to locate and retrieve the tape.

OTHER ADVENTURES WITH Tape Collage Art

→ Write sight words on the paper and have kids repeat the same process to add movement to learning.

→ Have kids tear several small pieces of tape and place them on their desks or tables. Have them place the tape pieces to indicate their answers on multiple-choice worksheets for a more hands-on experience.

Sticky-Note MURAL

→ You've used them to make your to-do list, but have you ever used those colorful sticky notes to create a work of art? Kids will get creative and work as a group to do just that in this lab.

MATERIALS
→ Sticky notes
→ Scissors
→ Pens/markers

PREPARE FOR YOUR ADVENTURE

1. Give a stack of sticky notes to each child participating in the activity.

2. Kids will draw guide lines on a stack of sticky notes (**fig. a**) to show where to cut to make a stack of a certain shape (e.g. one child may have a stack of triangles, one child may have squares, etc.).

3. Have kids cut their stacks of sticky notes using the guide lines drawn on the top note in order to create a stack of the same shape (**fig. b**). Make sure they keep the sticky tab intact and attached to the shapes.

Fig. a: Draw lines on sticky notes to mark a shape to be cut.

Fig. b: Cut out each shape, keeping the sticky tab intact.

BEGIN YOUR ADVENTURE

4. Have kids work together, starting in the center of the floor, to create a design using their sticky notes.

5. Place one sticky note in the center, and then have one kid place a ring of her sticky note shapes around the center note.

6. Have each kid in the group repeat this process, building outward from the center to create a mandala-like design **(fig. c)**.

7. As kids build their mural, they may find that they need to fill in some gaps and spaces by cutting new shapes. Let them continue working together to create their design until the open floor space is filled.

Fig. c: Use the different shapes to create a mural.

Maximize the Sensory Experience

→ Challenge kids to incorporate visual patterns into their design by alternating shapes or colors of sticky notes.

→ Call out a number of shapes each kid should place on the floor in the next ring of the design. If a ring isn't complete with that number of shapes, the next kid will have to continue that ring using her shape.

OTHER ADVENTURES WITH
Sticky Note Art

→ Have kids decide on a theme for their mural, writing related words, phrases, or sentences on their sticky notes.

→ Work on number or alphabet sequencing by having kids write consecutive numbers or letters on the sticky notes as they build outward (e.g. write 1 on the center sticky note, write 2s on the surrounding sticky notes, etc.)

PLAY DOUGH in a Bag

→ This color-mixing lab will take some strength and determination, but the end result makes it all worthwhile.

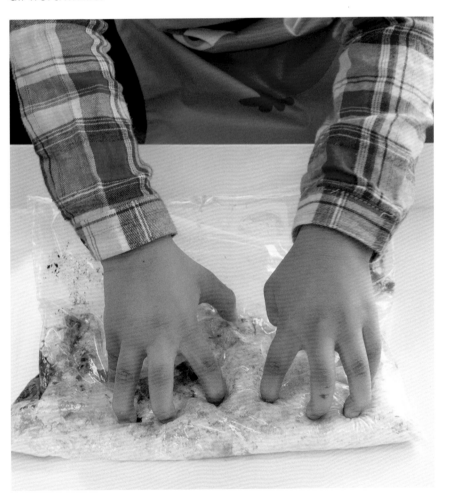

MATERIALS

- → large plastic zip-top bag
- → 1 cup (240 ml) of water
- → ¼ cup (60 ml) table salt
- → ½ teaspoon (2 ml) vegetable oil
- → ¾ cup (180 ml) flour
- → ½ tablespoon (7.5 ml) corn starch
- → Food coloring

PREPARE FOR YOUR ADVENTURE

1. Put all of the dry ingredients into the zip-top bag (salt, flour, and cornstarch). **(fig. a)**

2. Add the wet ingredients (oil, food coloring, and water). **(fig. b)**

3. Remove excess air from bag and seal the bag.

Fig. a: Pour the dry ingredients into the bag.

Fig. b: Add the wet ingredients to the bag.

BEGIN YOUR ADVENTURE

4. Have kids use their hands to squish and squeeze the bag to form the play dough **(fig. c)**.

5. Once the play dough forms, have kids remove it from the bag and knead it until it's completely mixed.

Fig. c: Mix the ingredients together to make a dough.

Something to Think About
→ Having kids work and play on a vertical surface is a great way to work on strengthening and stabilizing the upper body. Working in this position also promotes midline crossing and core strengthening.

Maximize the Sensory Experience

→ Add a few drops of essential oil to the bag to mix into the play dough (e.g. use lavender for calming, peppermint for alerting)

→ Try mixing colors by adding drops of different colors to the same bag and having kids mix with their hands.

OTHER ADVENTURES WITH
Play Dough in a Bag

→ Maximize the fine motor benefits of playing with play dough by hiding small objects in the dough for tiny fingers to find (e.g. buttons, coins, beads, etc.).

→ Try playing with your play dough in a different way by sticking it to mirrors or windows to create different designs.

GLUE RESIST
Secret Word

→ Some simple art supplies are all you'll need for this cool project where kids use their sense of touch to try to guess a secret word.

Fig. a: Use glue to write a word on the paper.

Fig. b: After the glue dries, color over the word with crayon.

Maximize the Sensory Experience

→ Sprinkle salt over the glue before it dries to add a gritty texture for an extra tactile experience when trying to guess the secret word.

→ Do this entire activity with a blindfold and have kids try to guess the word by feeling it and then staying blindfolded while they color until the word is revealed.

MATERIALS

→ Clear glue
→ Heavy paper (cardstock or construction paper)
→ Crayons or watercolor paint

PREPARE FOR YOUR ADVENTURE

1. One child or adult uses glue to write a word on the paper **(fig. a)**.

2. Let the paper dry until the glue is no longer sticky.

Fig. c: Reveal the secret word!

BEGIN YOUR ADVENTURE

3. Have a kid use his finger to trace over the glue to see if he can guess what the secret word is that has been written on the paper.

4. Next, have him color or paint the entire paper as creatively as he chooses **(fig. b)**.

5. See if he guessed correctly **(fig. c)**.

OTHER ADVENTURES WITH Secret Word Lab

→ Have a leader create a sentence by using the glue to write each individual word of that sentence on separate pieces of paper. As the kid paints or colors the paper to reveal each word, have him try to place the words in order to reveal the sentence.

→ Use the glue to create any design. The outcome will be a beautiful piece of art.

Shaving Cream COLOR MIXING

→ Experiment with beautiful, bright color combinations in this lab as kids squish, squeeze, and knead with their hands.

MATERIALS

→ Sealable plastic bag
→ Shaving cream
→ Packing tape or duct tape
→ Food coloring

PREPARE FOR YOUR ADVENTURE

1. Squirt shaving cream into a sealable bag, filling it about three-quarters of the way **(fig. a)**.

2. Place two drops of food coloring into one side of the bag **(fig. b)**.

3. Place two drops of another color of food coloring into the other side of the bag.

4. Seal the bag securely with tape.

Fig. a: Squirt shaving cream into the bag.

Fig. b: Place food coloring into one side of the bag.

BEGIN YOUR ADVENTURE

5. Have kids use their hands to mix and knead the bag to try to combine the two colors of food coloring (fig. c).

6. Kids should continue to mix until they see what new color has been created and until the entire bag has changed over to the new color.

7. Try the same activity again with two different colors.

Fig. c: Use your hands to mix the colors into the shaving cream.

Maximize the Sensory Experience

→ Add foam shapes to the bag. When kids are finished mixing the colors, they can use their fingers to try to find the shapes in their seek and find bag.

→ Try this activity using a large, sealable storage bag and have kids use their feet to mix the colors.

OTHER ADVENTURES WITH
Color Mixing

→ Before filling the bag with shaving cream, draw circular targets on it with permanent marker. Add a few buttons to the bag, along with the food coloring and shaving cream. Have kids mix the colors into the shaving cream, and then try to manipulate the buttons to match up with each of the circular targets

→ Have kids practice tracing letters on the bag with their fingers.

LARGER-THAN-LIFE Loom

→ This version of a weaving loom requires whole-body movement to create a huge, woven masterpiece. Kids get to work as a team to create an art project.

MATERIALS

→ Yarn
→ Long, narrow strips of fabric
→ 6-8 chairs with rungs on the back

PREPARE FOR YOUR ADVENTURE

1. Place 3 to 4 chairs side by side in a line at one end of the play space.

2. Place the other chairs side by side in a line at the opposite end of the play space.

3. Wrap yarn around the rungs on the backs of the chairs, stretching it across the play space to create a loom **(fig. a)**.

BEGIN YOUR ADVENTURE

4. Have kids work together to create a masterpiece by weaving the strips of fabric over and under the lengths of yarn **(fig. b)**.

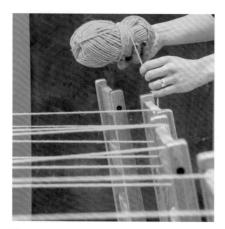

Fig. a: Wrap yarn around the backs of chairs, stretching it across the play space.

Fig. b: Weave strips of fabric into the yarn loom.

5. In order to reach the fabric strips to the opposite side of the loom, they'll need to crawl underneath the yarn loom, weaving the fabric through the loom over their heads **(fig. c)**.

Fig. c: Kids will crawl under the loom as they weave the fabric strips through the yarn.

Maximize the Sensory Experience

→ Try using the loom to create a pattern. Have kids work together to weave alternating colors of fabric through the yarn.

→ Experiment with creating the loom at a different height. If you create the loom lower to the ground, kids will have to lie on their backs and scoot under it as they weave their fabric. If you create a higher loom, kids will have to reach overhead to weave.

OTHER WAYS TO PLAY WITH

the Larger-than-Life Loom

→ When the weaving is complete, the kids can use the space underneath as a secret hideout. They can bring flashlights and books inside.

Fidget Tools

What is a fidget tool?

A fidget tool is a small toy or object that a kid (or adult) manipulates in her hands while reading, working, listening, or attending to another activity.

Fidget tools provide us with subtle movement and touch input that can help keep our bodies and minds calm, focused, and attentive. Movement is a powerful component of focus and problem solving. Fidget tools provide an outlet for that movement in a subtle way.

The need to fidget can be fulfilled by using something as complex as a commercially fabricated fidget toy with moving parts, or something as simple as a piece of paper that someone folds and unfolds with her fingers. While some teachers and parents may think of fidgets as being distracting, they can actually support students' attention and learning when they are introduced in a thoughtful, structured way.

Simple DIY Fidget Tools

→ Balloons filled with flour or play dough
→ Nuts and bolts
→ Sock filled with dry rice
→ Velcro stuck under a table or desk
→ Pipe cleaners
→ Flexible straws
→ Key rings
→ Hair bands
→ Pony beads on a large paper clip

WHOLE-BODY
Music Adventures

MUSIC CAN BE A WONDERFUL WAY
to target multiple sensory systems at once
as kids listen to, create, and move to different
beats and harmonies.

Homemade Percussion INSTRUMENTS

→ Creating a DIY percussion instrument is as easy as gathering up everyday objects you have around your home or classroom. Get creative as kids explore with sound!

MATERIALS

→ Variety of objects to use as drums (e.g. empty shoe box, coffee can, metal pot, etc.)
→ Variety of objects to use as drumsticks (e.g. popsicle sticks, twigs, whisk, pencils, spoons, etc.)

PREPARE FOR YOUR ADVENTURE

1. Search in and around your home for objects that would make good drums (**fig. a**).

2. Collect different objects to serve as drumsticks.

BEGIN YOUR ADVENTURE

3. Explore the different combinations of drums and drumsticks (**fig. b**).

4. Experiment with playing your drums fast and slow (**fig. c**).

5. Try beating your drum as hard as you can, and then beat it so softly that it barely makes a sound.

Fig. a: Provide different objects to use as drums and drumsticks.

Fig. b: Allow kids to choose which drums and drumsticks to try.

Fig. c: Experiment with the different sounds the drums and drumsticks make.

Maximize the Sensory Experience

→ Have an adult play a drum to accompany the kids' movements (e.g. jump, run, skip, or walk). Change the speed of the beat and watch how their movements respond to that change.

→ Have kids experiment with moving while they play their drums. Is it harder to play while moving?

→ Challenge auditory processing by playing a song and having kids keep beat with the music.

OTHER ADVENTURES WITH
Percussion Lab

→ Put together a band of drums with friends and notice the different sounds each drum makes.

→ Make a drum circle. Can each child make their own beat and maintain it while others join in?

Repeat-After-Me RHYTHM

→ Can kids follow along with a rhythm? Challenge those listening skills by helping them create their own rhythm sticks.

MATERIALS
→ Empty paper towel tubes
→ Fillers (e.g. pebbles, beads, rice, bells, dry pasta, etc.)
→ Clear packing tape
→ Embellishments (e.g. decorative paper, markers, crayons, washi tape, stickers, etc.)

PREPARE FOR YOUR ADVENTURE

1. Secure one end of the tube with packing tape.

2. Choose a filler and fill the tube halfway **(figs. a and b)**.

3. Secure the other end of the tube **(fig. c)**.

4. Decorate the tube to personalize **(fig. d)**.

BEGIN YOUR ADVENTURE

5. Assign one kid as the leader. Tell him to shake out a rhythm with the rhythm stick.

6. Have the rest of the group repeat the rhythm with their sticks **(fig. e)**.

7. Repeat, allowing each kid in the group to take a turn as the leader.

Fig. a: Provide small objects to use as filler materials.

Fig. b: Fill tubes halfway with small objects.

Fig. c: Secure the end of the tube and cover with colorful paper.

Fig. d: Decorate the tube using embellishments.

Fig. e: Take turns repeating one another's rhythms.

Maximize the Sensory Experience

→ Encourage kids to incorporate other body movements to create a unique rhythm (e.g. shake rhythm stick, stomp feet, tap rhythm stick on shoulder, etc.).

OTHER ADVENTURES WITH
Rhythm Sticks

→ Have kids close their eyes and shake their rhythm sticks one at a time. Can they guess what filler is inside?

→ Use rhythm sticks to play hand-clapping games (e.g. Miss Mary Mack, Patty Cake, etc.).

Rhythm DRIBBLE

→ Kids will keep the beat of the music in a totally new way, using an unexpected prop in this creative, gross-motor music lab.

MATERIALS
→ Basketball for each kid
→ Music with different rhythms (waltz, rap, classical, pop, etc.)

PREPARE FOR YOUR ADVENTURE

1. For each kid, find a basketball that is full of air and bounces easily (**fig. a**).

2. Compile a playlist of 3 to 5 songs that contain different rhythms.

3. Have kids practice bouncing and catching a basketball.

4. Have kids practice dribbling the basketball with control.

Fig. a: Provide a basketball to each child.

Fig. b: Bounce the ball along with the rhythm of a song.

BEGIN YOUR ADVENTURE

5. Listen to each of the songs in your playlist and notice the different rhythms.

6. Experiment with the rhythms by clapping along to each song.

7. Try bouncing the basketball along with the rhythm and talking about the beats **(fig. b)**. Are they fast or slow, short or long, soft or hard?

Maximize the Sensory Experience

→ Change the music quickly to see if the kids can react to the rhythm change while maintaining control of their basketballs.

→ Have kids experiment with moving while they bounce their basketballs. Is it harder to maintain the rhythm while moving?

OTHER ADVENTURES WITH
Rhythm Dribbling

→ See if each kid can pick out a different rhythm within the same song and play it while other kids play their individual rhythms.

→ Challenge bilateral coordination by having kids tap a rhythm with their feet or hands while dribbling to a faster rhythm with their balls.

Exploring Note VALUES

→ This movement-based music lab brings the concept of note values to life as kids make their way up and down a set of stairs based on the type of note they see.

MATERIALS

→ 10 to 12 notecards with drawings of the following musical notes: whole note, half note, and quarter note
→ A set of stairs

PREPARE FOR YOUR ADVENTURE

1. Gather the images of musical notes **(fig. a)**.

2. Make sure the stairs are clear of obstacles.

3. Place one musical note on each step.

BEGIN YOUR ADVENTURE

4. Talk about the value of each note with kid. Explain that a whole note is worth 4 counts, a half note is worth 2, and a quarter note is worth 1.

Fig. a: Gather images of musical notes.

Fig. b: Ascend the correct number of stairs based on the note value.

Maximize the Sensory Experience

→ After reaching the top of the stairs, have the child clap out the rhythm of the notes that she collected. For instance, if she collected a whole note, two half notes, and a quarter note, she would clap once and hold for four, then clap twice (holding each for two), and finally once.

→ Instead of using cards, call out the note names.

5. Explain that she will start at the bottom of the stairs with the first card and go up the number of stairs that represent the value of the note on that card **(fig. b)**. For example, if she sees a half note, she will go up 2 stairs. Have her pick up the cards as she reaches each stair **(fig. c)**.

6. She should continue to progress up the stairs, looking at the note on the card on each stair she lands on and ascending the number of stairs for that note's value until she reaches the top.

7. Repeat coming down the stairs.

Fig. c: When the child stops at the designated step, she picks another card.

OTHER ADVENTURES WITH
Exploring Note Values

→ If you don't have stairs, do this activity with lines of tape or chalk on the floor.

→ Use this activity to practice math facts by calling out equations and having the kids use the stairs to count out the answer, going up for addition and down for subtraction.

DIY Xylophone

→ What's even more fun than playing music? How about playing music with an instrument you make yourself. Kids will love creating their own xylophones in this unique music lab!

MATERIALS

→ Cardboard tubes (paper towel, toilet paper, wrapping paper, etc.)
→ Rubber bands
→ Yarn, ribbon, or embroidery floss

PREPARE FOR YOUR ADVENTURE

1. Cut your tubes so that you have 5 different lengths with about 1" (2.5 cm) difference in length between each tube **(fig. a)**.

2. Line the tubes up by length.

BEGIN YOUR ADVENTURE

3. Start with the two smallest tubes and use a rubber band to fasten them together **(fig. b)**. Put the rubber band around one tube, twist it so it makes a figure 8, and put the other loop around the next tube.

4. Put another rubber band around the other end of the two tubes in the same way.

Fig. a: Cut cardboard tubes at different lengths.

Fig. b: Use rubber bands to secure the tubes together.

Fig. c: Decorate the tubes.

Fig. d: Add a loop of yarn to the top tube.

5. Add the next biggest tube, attaching them using the same rubber band method. Keep going until you've added all of your tubes.

6. Have kids use yarn, ribbon, or embroidery floss to weave in and out of the xylophone tubes for decoration **(fig. c)**.

7. Add a loop of yarn, ribbon, or embroidery floss to the top tube so kids can wear their xylophones around their necks **(fig. d)**.

8. Have kids play their xylophones using pencils, markers, or chopsticks as sticks.

Maximize the Sensory Experience

→ Try filling the cardboard tubes with some rice, bells, or buttons and sealing each end to add to the auditory experience.

→ Have kids decorate their tubes using textured paper to maximize the tactile experience and change the sounds of their xylophones.

OTHER ADVENTURES WITH
DIY Xylophones

→ Try a repeat-after-me game where an adult or kid plays a certain rhythm on her xylophone and the rest of the group follows along.

→ Have a parade! Have kids march and move around the room in different ways (gallop, skip, giant steps, etc.) while playing xylophones.

PERFECT *Pitch*

→ Kids will use their bodies to show whether the notes they hear are high or low in this movement-based game about pitch.

MATERIALS

→ **Any instrument that you can use to play different note sounds (recorder, piano, harmonica, keyboard, etc.)**

PREPARE FOR YOUR ADVENTURE

1. Choose your instrument **(fig. a)**.

2. Have one kid stand in front of the group with the instrument.

BEGIN YOUR ADVENTURE

3. Explain to the group of kids that they will listen to a friend play a note on an instrument, and then they will then decide if the note they hear is high or low.

4. Play one sound as a starting point. For example, if you are on the piano, play a middle C.

Fig. a: Choose your instrument.

Fig. b: Play notes with different pitches and use movement to represent the pitch.

5. Explain to the kids that they will stand tall with their hands overhead if the pitch of the note is high, and they will crouch their bodies into a ball if the pitch is low.

6. Have the leader play a note and watch the kids perform the corresponding movement **(fig. b)**.

7. Repeat, using various notes.

Maximize the Sensory Experience

→ Try this activity in front of a mirror so kids can see their bodies move from one position to another, or have them try this with their eyes closed to challenge balance.

→ Have kids try to hum to match the pitch of the note played.

OTHER ADVENTURES WITH
Pitch Perfect

→ Grab a group of kids and play a game to see who can follow the pitch without making a mistake. If a kid stands tall when he should crouch, he is out of the game.

→ Increase the speed of the game. Play the notes quickly so kids have react with their bodies at a faster pace.

Sensory Activities for Small Spaces

YOU MAY BE A SCHOOL-BASED THERAPIST working in a cramped storage closet or a tiny corner of the hallway. Or maybe you're a teacher who knows how important it is to get those kiddos up and moving, but you have no space to do it. Maybe you're a parent whose little one craves movement and other sensory input, but you just don't have the room for lots of equipment and large toys.

Kids need to move and bounce and crash and jump and spin and roll but often, there is no space for them to do it in. The following ideas are quick and easy sensory activities that you can pack up and store away when you're not using them. They'll help you infuse a little movement and sensory input into kids' daily routines.

1. Wall push-ups or chair push-ups

2. Bean bags

3. Animal walks/dinosaur stomps

4. Squeeze balls or sensory balloons

5. Play dough

6. Bubble wrap

7. Whistles and kazoos

8. Flashlights

9. Streamers

10. Seek and find bottles

UNIT

7

WHOLE-BODY, Hands-On GEOGRAPHY PLAY

WHAT BETTER WAY FOR KIDS TO LEARN
about the world around them than through whole-body
sensory play? These hands-on, movement-infused labs
are great for introducing landforms, different locations
around the globe, and directionality.

Feet IN THE Sand

→ Spice up a simple sensory bin by letting kids dig in with their toes. Then, have them sort the animals by identifying where they live.

MATERIALS
→ Large plastic bin
→ Play sand
→ Small, plastic animals (ocean and land animals)
→ 2 smaller containers for categorizing animals

PREPARE FOR YOUR ADVENTURE

1. Fill a large, plastic bin with sand.

2. Label the two smaller containers as land and water, and place them near the sand bin.

3. Bury the plastic animals in the sand.

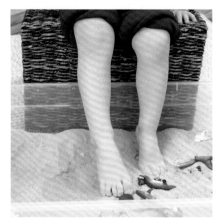

Fig. a: Dig into the sand using both feet.

Fig. b: Pick up the animals with your toes and place them into the correct containers.

BEGIN YOUR ADVENTURE

4. Have kids take off their shoes and socks and sit in chairs around the edge of the large plastic bin.

5. Tell them to use their feet and toes to dig into the sand to find the buried animals **(fig. a)**.

6. Tell them to pull an animal out of the sand with their toes and decide whether the animal lives in the water or on land **(fig. b)**. Have them place the animals in the correct containers using only their toes.

Maximize the Sensory Experience

→ Try the same activity using water, bird seed, or shaving cream instead of sand.

→ The deeper the sand, the greater the resistance will be for additional strengthening of those little toes.

OTHER ADVENTURES WITH
Feet in the Sand

→ Use the same activity to explore other habitats (e.g. saltwater vs. freshwater, forest vs. desert, etc.)

→ Using their toes, have kids practice writing words in the sand that relate to the animals or their habitats.

Strategic LANDFORM

→ Working as a team on this cooperative, problem-solving lab is a unique way to learn about the features of different landforms.

MATERIALS

→ Landform words and pictures printed on separate pieces of paper

→ Carpet squares or large squares of heavy cardboard or paper, approximately 1' x 1' (30 cm x 30 cm)

PREPARE FOR YOUR ADVENTURE

1. Introduce the various landforms, describing their features and showing pictures.

2. Hang the landform words and pictures in different places around the play space.

3. Designate a starting point for your game. Have kids stand on their carpet/cardboard squares in a single-file line with the leader positioned on the starting point.

Fig. a: Work together to move across carpet squares, cardboard, or paper.

Fig. b: Move the squares to move around the room as a team without touching the floor.

Maximize the Sensory Experience

→ Have kids take off their shoes and socks and use squares with different textures to maximize the tactile experience.

→ Instead of providing a written list, call out a sequence of 3 or 4 landforms and have kids remember the list as they make their way around the room to the different targets.

BEGIN YOUR ADVENTURE

4. Give kids a written list of landforms, instructing the kids that they have to work together to get their whole group from the starting point to each of the landforms in the correct sequence without stepping off of their squares **(fig. a)**.

5. Allow kids to figure out how to move their carpet squares, share carpet squares with their teammates, and other strategies to move around the room without touching the floor **(fig. b)**.

6. Once they have completed the sequence and reached all of the designated landforms **(fig. c)**, have everyone return to the starting point to try a new sequence of landforms. Can they complete the exercise in a different way?

Fig. c: The kids must reach each landform picture in the correct sequence.

OTHER ADVENTURES WITH
Strategic Landforms

→ Work on other map concepts with the same game. For example, challenge kids to move 3 squares north, 5 squares west, etc. until they reach an endpoint.

→ As the group reaches each landform poster, have one team member read the description or features of the landform to the group.

LAB 49

DIRECTIONality

→ Whole-body movement is one of the best ways to teach any new concept or skill. As kids follow the arrows in this fun game, they'll gain a better understanding of north, south, east, and west.

MATERIALS
→ 8 pieces of construction paper or other heavy-duty paper
→ Sheet of notebook paper
→ Pencil
→ Scissors

PREPARE FOR YOUR ADVENTURE

1. Introduce the directionality concepts of north, south, east, and west. Mark the directions somewhere in the room (e.g. put an N on one wall, W on another, etc).

2. Place arrows in a line on the floor facing in different directions toward the north, west, east, and south walls **(fig. a)**.

3. Have a kid stand behind the first arrow and state which direction she is facing **(fig. b)**.

Fig. a: Place arrows in a line on the floor facing different directions.

Fig. b: Stand behind the first arrow and state which direction you are facing.

BEGIN YOUR ADVENTURE

4. Have kids jump from arrow to arrow, one at a time, calling out the directions that they are facing.

5. Next, draw a sequence of 8 arrows on a piece of paper, all facing in different directions.

6. Give a kid the paper and see if he can replicate the sequence you drew using the arrows on the floor.

7. Encourage him to jump from arrow to arrow, calling out this new sequence of directions **(fig. c)**.

8. Repeat with different direction sequences.

Fig. c: Jump from arrow to arrow, calling out the sequence of directions.

Maximize the Sensory Experience

→ Change up the challenge and write directional terms on the cards. See if the kids can arrange the arrows correctly.

→ Instead of providing a written list, call out a sequence of 3 to 4 directions. Kids should arrange the arrows and complete the jumping sequence—from memory.

OTHER ADVENTURES WITH Directionality

→ Work on other directional concepts. For example, challenge kids to move left, right, forward, and backward.

→ Generalize this skill to map reading. Provide a large map and have kids start behind a sequence of arrows. Have them name a landmark that is in the direction that the arrow is pointing. For example, if he is in the United States behind an arrow pointing north, he may say Canada.

MAP Sensory Bin

→ Kids will put their hands to work to dig for different landmarks on a map in this twist on a tactile sensory bin.

MATERIALS

→ Storage container with a clear bottom
→ Tactile bin filler (e.g. beads, dry rice, sand, dry beans, etc.)
→ A map
→ Tape

PREPARE FOR YOUR ADVENTURE

1. Tape the map to the bottom of the container on the outside so the map is facing upward and can be seen in the container **(fig. a)**.

2. Fill the storage container with the preferred filler **(fig. b)**.

BEGIN YOUR ADVENTURE

3. Have kids use their hands to move the filler around in the container to reveal different parts of the map **(fig. c)**.

4. Encourage kids to talk about what they find (e.g. cities, states, countries, landmarks, etc.). **(fig. d)**

Fig. a: Tape a map to the bottom of a clear container.

Fig. b: Fill the container with a tactile bin filler.

Fig. c: Use your hands to move the filler around inside the container to reveal parts of the map.

Fig. d: Identify the cities, states, countries, or landmarks as they are uncovered.

Maximize the Sensory Experience

→ Change up the bin fillers to provide different tactile experiences.

→ Call out a certain location for kids to find on the map and see if they can find it without help.

OTHER ADVENTURES WITH
Your Map Sensory Bin

→ Tape images of other learning concepts (e.g. letters, numbers, shapes, colors, etc.) to the bottom of the container and have kids find and recognize them.

→ After kids find each letter, number, or shape, have them trace the figures in the sensory bin with their fingers.

THE WORLD Around Me

→ Kids will get a closer look at where they live in this unique challenge. This is a great way to teach kids about their homes, their neighborhoods, their countries, and more.

PREPARE FOR YOUR ADVENTURE

1. Roll balls of play dough to represent each place where kids live (a small ball for their house, a slightly bigger ball for their street, slightly bigger for their city, etc.) **(fig. a)**.

2. Place balls of play dough at different spots on a table top.

3. Place lines of tape down on the table to make roads connecting the balls of play dough **(fig. b)**.

4. Place the corresponding image cards into the balls of play dough (the house image should go in the smallest ball, next the street image, then the city image, etc.).

BEGIN YOUR ADVENTURE

5. Explain that each ball of play dough represents a different aspect of the world we live in. Discuss each of the images.

MATERIALS
→ Play dough
→ Images or photos of where kids live (e.g. house, street, city, state, country, continent, planet, etc.)
→ 1 Straw
→ 1 Ping pong ball
→ Painter's tape or masking tape

Fig. a: Roll balls of play dough and place them on the table.

Fig. b: Place lines of tape on the surface to connect the balls of play dough.

Maximize the Sensory Experience

→ Try this same activity while kids lie on their bellies or on hands and knees on the floor for added strengthening and breath-control practice.

→ Use textured washi tape to make the roads and have the kids trace them to the destination using their fingers.

6. Have the kid use the straw to blow the ping pong ball along the taped lines, starting at his house. As he reaches each stop on the journey through his world, have him stop, take a breath, and provide details about that stop (e.g. I live in a white house or I live in the city of Bedford) **(fig. c)**.

7. Have him continue until he gets to the largest aspect of his world, the planet he lives on, and then re-cap all of the stops along the way.

Fig. c: Blow the ping pong ball along the tape, stopping to make note of each picture.

OTHER ADVENTURES WITH
The World Around Me

→ Use this method of learning through movement to practice identifying shapes, colors, numbers, and letters. Place pictures of each concept in the play dough balls and complete the activity the same way.

→ Use the play dough balls to introduce and practice the concept of size. Have kids place the play dough balls in order from biggest to smallest.

Something to Think About
→ Blowing through a straw is a great way to strengthen the muscles of the mouth for lip closure when drinking or eating, as well as overall voice production. Blowing is also very calming as it encourages deep breathing and long exhalations.

GLOBE TOSS Geography

→ Inspire kids to get familiar with the globe by putting it right into their hands. All you need is a beach ball and a marker to get started.

MATERIALS
→ Beach ball
→ Permanent marker
→ Globe or a world map for reference

PREPARE FOR YOUR ADVENTURE

1. Blow up the beach ball.

2. Using the marker, draw a representation of the globe, as accurately as possible, using only the outlines of the continents (**fig. a**).

3. Give it a few minutes to dry.

BEGIN YOUR ADVENTURE

4. Have kids stand approximately 10' (3 m) away from an adult or another kid.

5. Have kids play catch with the ball (**fig. b**).

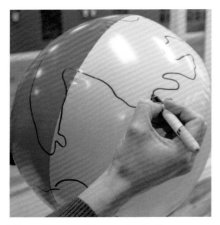

Fig. a: Draw a globe on the ball.

Fig. b: Play catch with the ball.

Maximize the Sensory Experience

→ Try tapping the beach ball into the air for a certain number of times between players to practice hand-eye coordination and body awareness.

→ Call out a large landmark and see if the kid can catch the beach ball right on target.

6. When a kid catches the beach ball, have him look at one of his hands and tell you a geographical feature that this hand is touching (fig. c).

7. Continue tossing the beach ball and discussing the major geographical features.

Fig. c: When you catch the ball, identify a feature of the globe one hand is touching.

OTHER ADVENTURES WITH
Your Globe Toss

→ You can use the beach ball for different academic concepts (e.g. draw letters, numbers, shapes, etc.) and play the same way.

→ After kids determine a landmark on the beach ball, have them state a fact about that geographical area (e.g. there are 50 states in the United States, The Alps are a mountain range in Switzerland, etc.).

Resources

The Inspired Treehouse
theinspiredtreehouse.com

Sensory Processing 101
By Dayna Abraham,
Claire Heffron, Pamela Braley,
and Lauren Drobnjak
sensoryprocessing101.com

The OT Toolbox
theottoolbox.com

Your Therapy Source
www.yourtherapysource.com

Miss Jaime OT
www.missjaimeot.com

Kids Play Space
www.kidsplayspace.com.au

Growing Hands-On Kids
www.growinghandsonkids.com

Pink Oatmeal
www.pinkoatmeal.com

Your Kids OT
www.yourkidsot.com

The Pocket Occupational Therapist
www.pocketot.com

Dinosaur Physical Therapy
dinopt.com

About the Authors

Claire Heffron is a practicing pediatric occupational and physical therapist. She holds a master of science in occupational therapy from The University of North Carolina and has been practicing in public and specialized school-based settings for 10 years.

Lauren Drobnjak graduated from Youngstown State University with a bachelor's of science in physical therapy. She has practiced for more than 15 years in both clinical and school-based settings.

ABOUT THE INSPIRED TREEHOUSE

Together, Claire and Lauren run theinspiredtreehouse.com, an online community serving therapists, parents, and teachers. They believe that with a little help, kids can build strong, healthy bodies and minds through play. They feature easy-to-implement activities that are designed to promote all kinds of developmental skills for kids. As pediatric occupational and physical therapists, they are also passionate about sharing information, tips, and strategies to help their readers conquer the common developmental roadblocks that come up for kids. They believe that the more parents, teachers, and caregivers know about child development and wellness, the better off kids are! Visit their website to learn more: theinspiredtreehouse.com

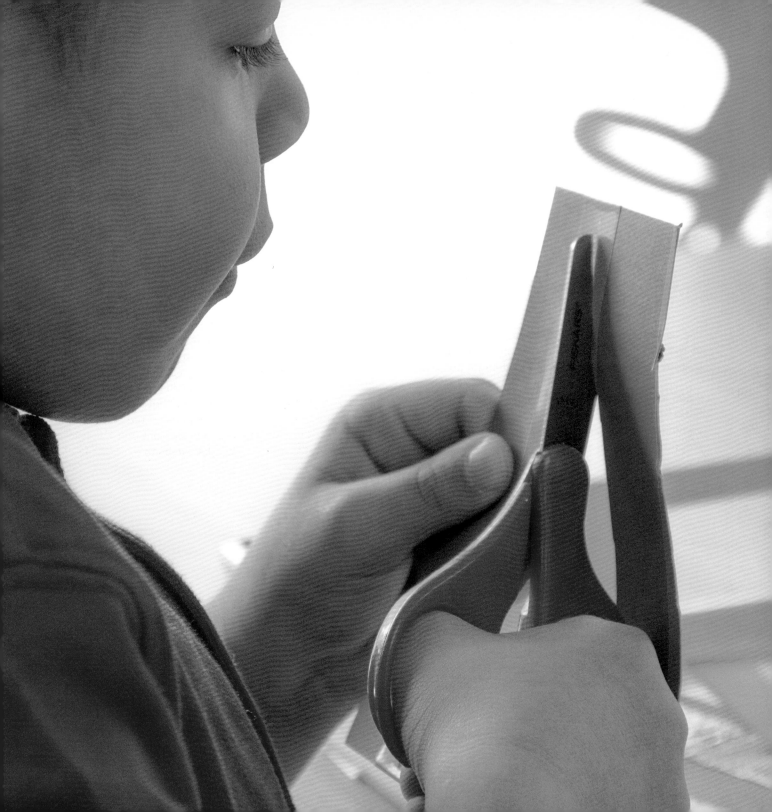